Betsy Lurvink

FORTE PUBLISHERS

Contents

ISBN 90 5877 260 8
Fourth printing January 2004

This is a publication from
Forte Publishers BV
P.O. Box 1394
3500 BJ Utrecht
The Netherlands

For more information about the creative books available from Forte Uitgevers:
www.hobby-party.com

Publisher: Marianne Perlot
Editor: Hanny Vlaar
Photography and digital image editing:
Fotografie Gerhard Witteveen, Apeldoorn, the Netherlands
Cover design: Studio Herman Bade BV, Baarn, the Netherlands
Inner design: Elgraphic+DTQP bv, Schiedam, the Netherlands
Translation: TextCase, Groningen, the Netherlands

Preface	3
Techniques	4
Step-by-step	5
Materials	6
Cards on the cover and page 1	7
For him and her	8
Children playing	11
Say it with flowers	14
Long live the holidays	16
Nice big cards	19
Triptych cards	22
A day out	26
Card on page 3	27
Folded cards	28
Babies and elves	31

Preface

Eyelets in different colours and shapes, various Sizzix dies, vellum and attractive cutting sheets by Marij Rahder are the ingredients for the cards in this book. You can rotate and slide them, or even play with them.

The cutting sheets consist of the individual parts of the pictures, such as little dolls with separate arms and legs, animals with separate tails and some great moveable objects. You can join the separate parts together using eyelets and then stick them on the card. You can really do things with these cards.

I hope you can use these cards to please many a birthday boy or girl, to cheer up a sick person, to congratulate somebody who is celebrating an anniversary, or just to cheer somebody up.

So, lets begin!

Betsy

Thanks
Gerard for all the typing, Annelies for cutting the sheets, Marij and René Rahder for the excellent cooperation and the pretty cutting sheets and Marianne Perlot for giving me the opportunity to write this book.

Techniques

1. Eyelets

You can punch the small, coloured eyelets into the card using the toolkit.

You can use the eyelets for the following:

1. To attach separate parts of a picture together so that they can move and rotate.
2. To attach shapes (for example, from a Sizzix die-cutter) or paper (for example, vellum) to a card without using glue or tape.
3. To decorate a card using suitable eyelet shapes, such as hearts, stars, snow crystals, apples, flowers or leaves.
4. To thread a pretty coloured thread or ribbon through a card for decoration.
5. To hang a card, label or a part of a pattern on a card.

2. Fixing eyelets

Punch a hole where you wish to have an eyelet using the hollow pipe from the toolkit and a hammer. Press the eyelet through the hole, possibly using an eyelet shape or another object. Turn the card over and hit the eyelet using the striking tool from the toolkit and a hammer to close the back. A piece of hardboard can be used to rest the card on when hitting the eyelet (see page 27).

3. Sizzix die-cutter

See the photograph and explanation on pages 26 and 27.

4. Cutting sheets

The cutting sheets which Marij has made for this book consist of the individual parts of pictures which you can connect together using eyelets. The moving parts must first be strengthened. Strengthen them as follows:

Roughly cut out the part to be strengthened. Stick it on (white) card (160 gram) using glue. Allow the glue to dry and then accurately cut out the shape. Next, punch the holes for the eyelets (see point 2).

5. Vellum

Vellum is a transparent, coloured and sometimes decorated paper which can be used on a background card. It is difficult to glue vellum to a card without the glue being seen. Eyelets are an excellent way to attach the vellum to the card in a decorative way.

6. Coluzzle cutting template

I have used Coluzzle templates for a number of cards. The best way to cut along the grooves is to use the special Coluzzle cutting mat and the pivoting Coluzzle knife. Start from the outside when counting the grooves.

Carry out the following:

First, place a piece of scrap paper on the cutting mat, so that the cuts will not fray. Next,

1. Materials – stick the children on 160 gram card.

2. Punch the motorbike, cut out the children and punch the four holes.

3. Use eyelets to attach the vellum to the card and the children to the motorbike.

4. Stick the motorbike on the card. Add the wheels and make everything 3D.

place the card on the cutting mat and place the cutting template you wish to use in the correct position on the card. Stick the Coluzzle template down using non-permanent adhesive tape. Hold the knife vertically in the groove you wish to cut and slide the knife carefully along the groove. Cut through the remaining piece after you have removed the template. This is an easy way to cut frames and borders in the card.

7. 3D cutting

Marij has designed the cutting sheets so that the parts you need to make 3D pictures have been drawn in steps. Cut the pieces out and puff them up slightly. Stick pieces of foam tape behind them and stick them in the correct position. You can, of course, also raise the pictures by using 3D glue.

Materials

- ❑ Marij Rahder cutting sheets: nos. S2300 to E2315
- ❑ Square cards (Artoz, Kars)
- ❑ Card: Artoz (A) and Canson Mi-Teintes (C)
- ❑ Embossed paper (Kars)
- ❑ Happy Color card (HC) (Kars/Romak)
- ❑ Gallery cards (Kars)
- ❑ Paper – Artoz 100 grams (Kars)
- ❑ Vellum: Marianne Design and Pergamano
- ❑ Sizzix die-cutter and dies (Kars)

- ❑ Coluzzle templates, pivoting knife and cutting mat (Kars)
- ❑ Eyelets in different colours and the toolkit (Kars)
- ❑ Eyelet shapes in different colours (Kars)
- ❑ Photo corner figure punch (Kars)
- ❑ Corner punches and line border punches (Kars)
- ❑ Alphabet punch and number punch (Kars)
- ❑ Cutting mat, knife and cutting ruler

- ❑ 3D scissors, foam tape and photo glue (Kars)
- ❑ Identi-pens: red and black (Kars)
- ❑ Sticker sheets: decorative borders and texts (Kars)
- ❑ Wire & Wire 26 gauge/0.45 mm wire
- ❑ Round wood (Ø5 mm and Ø8 mm)
- ❑ Cord and ribbon (Kars)

Cards on the cover and page 1

- Cutting sheet no. S2308
- Card: 26 x 13 cm – mango (A575)
- Card: A4 – yellow (A275) and birch green (A305)
- Vellum: rose fairy
- A4 card: orange (HC08)
- Sizzix die-cutter and motorbike die
- Eyelet shapes (snow crystal, heart and flower) and eyelet toolkit

Together on the motorbike (cover and page 5)

Punch out the motorbike. Strengthen the boy and girl and cut them out. Use an eyelet to attach the foot of the boy to the motorbike at the same height as the pedals. Use an eyelet to attach the girl to the saddle. Cut a piece of vellum (13 x 13 cm) and use eyelets and heart shapes to attach it to the card. Stick the motorbike to the vellum using pieces of foam tape. The children can now move on the motorbike. Use orange eyelets to attach the spokes to the card. Make the pictures 3D to hide the eyelets for the boy and girl.

The first kiss (card on page 1)

This card consists of two separate parts. Cut the outer card (25 x 12.5 cm, see diagram on page 20) and cut out the opening. Also cut a green inner card (25 x 12.5 cm, see the diagram on page 10) and fold this according to the diagram. Put the cards together and use a pencil to mark the place where slightly more than half of the opening must be cut out of the green card. Cut out the log with flowers for the background from the cutting sheet and stick it exactly under the opening. Strengthen the boy and the girl and cut them out. Use an eyelet to attach the feet under the girl and then use an eyelet to attach the girl at shoulder height next to the opening. Stick the parts of the card together and make the girl 3D. This will hide the eyelets, but the girl will still be able to move. Make the boy 3D and stick him to the narrow, folded strip using photo glue. Decorate the card. The card can now be opened to create depth and allow the boy and the girl to kiss each other.

For him and her

These cards are excellent for special

occasions.

What you need
- ❑ *Cutting sheets: nos. S2300, E2311 and E2312*
- ❑ *Card: 26 x 13 cm – fawn (A241), crimson (A549) and pink (A481)*
- ❑ *Card: 21 x 15 cm – snow white (HC 10) and red embossed*
- ❑ *Sizzix die-cutter and bus and motorbike dies*
- ❑ *Vellum: rose fairy and pink clouds*
- ❑ *Eyelets, shapes and toolkit*
- ❑ *Square Coluzzle template*
- ❑ *Red Identi-pen and hearts line border punch*
- ❑ *Border and text stickers, moving eyes*

1. Just married
Cut a piece of vellum (13 x 13 cm) and use pink eyelets and flower shapes to attach it to the fawn card. Punch the bus out of red card. Use eyelets to attach the arms to the upper bodies of the man and woman (the legs are not used) and cut away the woman's hat. Slide them into the opening of the bus and stick them in place using photo glue. Thread three differently coloured eyelets to three pieces of cord to make tin cans and keep them on the cord using small wooden beads. Use the punch to make a hole in the middle of the bus. Thread the cords through the hole and stick them to the card using adhesive tape. Stick the bus to the vellum using pieces of foam tape. Stick the red eyes and the text "Just Married" on the bus. Thread a red cord through the eyelets.

2. Voluptuous dancer
Cut a piece of vellum (15 x 10.5 cm) and use pink eyelets and heart shapes to attach it to the card. Cut the background from the cutting sheet and stick it on the snow white card under the vellum to create a watermark effect. Use eyelets to stick the separate parts of the dancer together. Make an incision in the card at the same height as the neck. Stick the neck through the incision and then attach the bottom eyelet to the card. Make the dancer 3D, but leave the middle eyelet free to suggest movement.

3. Invitation
Use the square Coluzzle template (grooves 1 and 2) to make a frame. Stick this on the square card (26 x 13 cm) and decorate it with a decorative border. Use the Coluzzle template (grooves 5 and 6) to make a smaller square and

use two eyelets to attach it to the card. Stick the kitchen utensils on the card.

4. Happy 50ᵗʰ birthday

Make a card (32 x 13 cm) and then cut away the top half. Punch the heart border out of red card using the border punch and stick it inside the card. Use the square Coluzzle template (groove 5) to cut an opening in the card. Use the template (grooves 4 and 5) to make a frame and stick this around the opening. Decorate the card with a border sticker. Attach the separate parts of the woman together and punch an eyelet through her chest to attach her to the card, so that she can move in every direction. Cut out the kitchen utensils and stick them on the card. Colour the text and "50" red using the Identi-pen and stick them on the card.

5. Speed merchant

Cut a wavy piece of cream card for the street and stick it on the square card (26 x 13 cm). Punch the motorbike out of red embossed card. Use eyelets to connect the separate parts of the sportsman together. Place him on the motorbike and stick all the parts to the card using foam tape. Cut the sports bag and the equipment out and stick the bag on the card. Raise the bag and place the racket, shoes and ball in the bag. Use red eyelets to attach the spokes in the wheels. Cut out the roller skate. Stick it on red card and cut it out with a small border. Attach an eyelet in the shoe and the card and attach the shoe to the card using a green cord. Finally, stick the text sticker and "50" on the card.

Continued from page 11

4. The kite

Cut a piece of dark chestnut card (13 x 5 cm) and cut it in a curve. Stick this at the bottom of the yellow card (13 x 13 cm). Stamp the background scene using blue stamp-pad ink. Use eyelets to connect the strengthened parts of the children together. Also strengthen the kite and the skateboard. Punch a couple of red eyelets in the wheels of the skateboard. Make a long spiral from Wire & Wire 26 gauge wire and stick it to the hand and the kite using foam tape. Add a couple of yellow eyelets and red star shapes to the card.

Children playing

Cards to play with.

What you need:
- ❏ *Cutting sheet no. E2310*
- ❏ *Card: 26 x 13 cm – yellow (A275), azure (A393), sky blue (A391) and dark chestnut (C501)*
- ❏ *Card: A4 – yellow (A275)*
- ❏ *Vellum: pale blue with blue waves and text*
- ❏ *Eyelets, toolkit and shapes: flower and snow crystal*
- ❏ *Sizzix die-cutter and the cart, sailing boat and car dies*
- ❏ *Photograph corner figure punch (curl)*
- ❏ *Wire & Wire 26 gauge wire and a thin knitting needle*
- ❏ *Background stamp and blue stamp-pad ink*

1. Congratulations

Make a yellow double card (15 x 13 cm). Attach vellum of the same size to the card using eyelets and snow crystal shapes in the corners. Strengthen the parts of the boy and use eyelets to connect the parts together. Attach the boy to the card using the eyelet for the right leg. Punch the cart twice out of red card. Stick the first cart to the card using glue and use foam tape for the second cart. Stick the toys on the card. Twist Wire & Wire 26 gauge around the knitting needle to make a long spiral and use adhesive tape to stick it to the cart and the strengthened balloon. Stick the kite on red card and cut it out leaving a border. Use an eyelet to attach it to the card.

2. Your driving licence

Cut a piece of vellum (13 x 13 cm) and use eyelets to attach it to a sky blue double card. Punch the car out of dark blue embossed card and stick it on the vellum using foam tape. Place the red eyelet shapes behind the headlights. Cut out the strengthened parts of the girl and use eyelets to connect them together. Cut out the dog and place it in the car with the girl.

3. Many congratulations

Cut out a piece of vellum (13 x 13 cm) and attach it to an azure double card using eyelets and flower shapes. Punch the sailing boat out of dark blue embossed card and stick it on the vellum using foam tape. Cut out the strengthened parts of the girl and the boy and use eyelets to connect the parts together. The girl is attached to the card using the eyelet for the left shoulder and the boy is attached to the card using the eyelet for the right shoulder, so that they can show off their antics. Stick the plane at the top of the card.

Continued on page 10

1.

2.

3.

4.

Say it with flowers

Home-made card are a creative way of showing somebody your feelings

What you need:

- ❑ *Cutting sheets: nos. S2307, S2308, E2314 and E2315*
- ❑ *Card: 26 x 13 cm – dark blue (A417) and pine green (A339)*
- ❑ *Card: 32 x 16 cm – crimson (A549)*
- ❑ *Card: 25 x 12½ cm – sea green (HC04) and carnival red (HC03)*
- ❑ *100 gram card: pastel green (A331) and pastel blue (A413)*
- ❑ *Pieces of card: sunny yellow (A247), apple green (HC09) and orange (HC08)*
- ❑ *Yellow embossed card*
- ❑ *Safari card (tiger print)*
- ❑ *Coluzzle templates: square and rectangle*
- ❑ *Eyelets, shapes and toolkit*
- ❑ *Sizzix die-cutter and the fence and branch with leaves dies*
- ❑ *Line border punches: flower and leaf*
- ❑ *Apple punch*
- ❑ *Green cord*

1. In love

Cut a piece of card (13.8 x 13.8 cm) from 100 gram card. Punch out the decorative border using the line border punch starting with mark seven, so that they fit nicely along the sides. Punch the fence out of carnival red card and stick it on the light blue card. Strengthen the boy and the girl and cut them out. Use eyelets to attach them to the light blue card. Punch an eyelet with a heart shape between the boy and the girl and in the four corners. Stick the light blue card on the dark blue card.

2. Get well soon

Make an orange card (30 x 14 cm). Cut out a rectangle using groove 5 of the Coluzzle template and cut the frame out of light green card using grooves 4 and 5. Stick a piece of green card behind the opening using foam tape. Cut out the stool, the mouse and the bunch of flowers and stick them on the green background. Stick a monkey's head in the corner. Use eyelets to connect the parts of the snake together and have it coil through the leaves. Punch the apples out of yellow card. Colour the letter stickers black using the Identi-pen. Divide the text "Get well soon" between the apples and stick them on the card using pieces of foam tape. Add a couple of green eyelets and yellow apple shapes and a border sticker to the card.

3. Swinging animals

Cut the tree out of cutting sheet S2307 and stick it on the card. Strengthen the ropes, the lion, the elephant and the snake. Let the lion hold a bunch of flowers in its claws. Use eyelets to attach the tails. Punch the eyelets in the separate parts of the snake and connect them together with an attractive cord. Cut the ropes through the middle and attach one end to the head of the lion and the other end to the head of the elephant using glue or pieces of strong adhesive tape. Use eyelets to attach the ropes with the pulleys to the tree. Strengthen the large leaves and use eyelets to attach them to the card. Coil the snake around the leaves and stick the head to the card using a piece of foam tape. Punch the fence out of jungle paper and stick the ends to the card using photo glue so that it is slightly open.

4. A little pick-me-up

Cut two squares out of the card using groove 6 of the Coluzzle template and cut the square borders out of yellow embossed card using grooves 5 and 6. Strengthen the frog and the webbed feet. Use eyelets to attach the feet to the card. Stick the yellow borders around the squares. Cut a piece of yellow embossed card (12.5 x 12.5 cm). Punch the eyelets in the card and thread a cord through them. Stick the ends of the cord to the inside of the card using a piece of double-sided foam tape. Stick the frogs, the flower and the sticker on the card. Punch the leaves out and stick them on the card.

Long live the holidays

A holiday card is always nice, even if you haven't been on holiday.

What you need:
- ❏ *Cutting sheets: nos. S2307, E2310, E2314 and E2315*
- ❏ *Card: dark blue (A417), lobster red (A545), crimson (A549), dark green (A309), bright yellow (C400), dark green (C448), ivory (C111) and almond green (C480)*
- ❏ *Embossed paper: A4 – dark blue*
- ❏ *Happy Color paper (various colours)*
- ❏ *Pieces of jungle paper*
- ❏ *100 gram card: azure (A393)*
- ❏ *Eyelets, shapes and toolkit*
- ❏ *Coluzzle templates: oval and rectangle*
- ❏ *Line border punches: leaf and elegance*
- ❏ *Stamp (lake) and Versamark ink*
- ❏ *Sizzix die-cutter and bath, tree, parasol, canoe and cart dies*
- ❏ *Balloon punch*

General information

The cards on this page consist of an inner card (Canson) and an outer card (Artoz) which are cut to the correct size from A4 sheets. Always fold the inner card three times: make a mountain fold in the middle and a valley fold on both sides of the mountain fold. The exact sizes are given for each card. Finish the inner card before sticking it in the outer card.

1. Just relax

Make a dark blue card (15 x 13.5 cm). Make the same size card from light blue card and punch a decorative border in the left and right-hand sides using the line border punch (elegance). Fold a mountain fold in the middle and a valley fold 5 cm on both sides of this fold. Cut out half of an oval in the middle of the card using groove 2 of the oval Coluzzle template. Make a border from yellow paper using grooves 1 and 2 of the Coluzzle template and stick it on the card. Stamp the lakes. Punch the bath out of dark blue embossed card. Cut out two strengthened frogs and use an eyelet to attach them to the card. Use two eyelets with heart shapes to attach the bath to the card. Cut out the other strengthened frogs and the windbreak and use eyelets to attach them to the card. Punch the parasol out of two colours of yellow card, make it 3D and stick it on the card. Stick the text sticker on the card. Cut the background out of cutting sheet S2302 and stick it in the middle of the dark blue outer card. Finally, stick the inner card in the outer card.

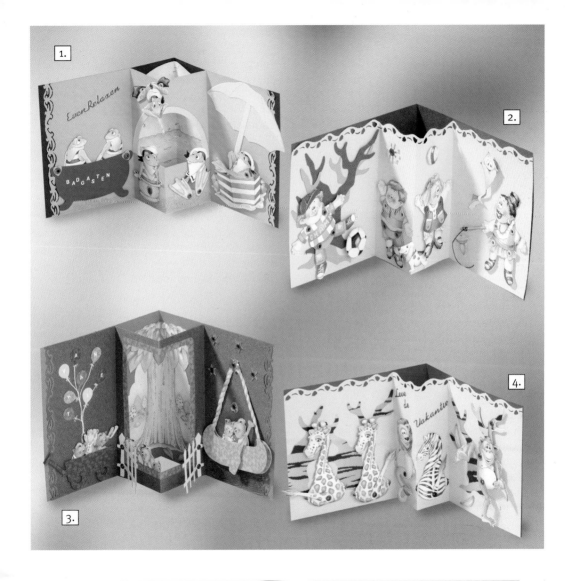

2. Children playing

Make a dark green card (15 x 12.5 cm). Make the same size card from yellow card and punch a decorative border in the top using the leaf line border punch. Fold a mountain fold in the middle and a valley fold 5 cm on both sides of this fold. Punch a tree out of light green and dark green card and stick them on the card with one slightly on top of the other. Cut out four strengthened children and use eyelets to connect the pieces together, except one arm, and then use one eyelet to attach them to the card. Stick the spinning top, the kite, the dog and the ball on the card using pieces of foam tape. Also add a red eyelet with a yellow snow crystal shape. Stick the card in the outer card. All the children on the card can now move and all the arms and legs can be placed in any position you wish. This makes it a card you can really play with.

3. Holiday

Make a lobster red double card (15 x 15 cm). Cut a piece of dark green card (15 x 15 cm) and punch a decorative border in the left and right-hand sides. Make a mountain fold in the middle and a valley fold 6 cm from this fold on both sides. Cut out the opening using groove 3 of the rectangular Coluzzle template. Make a border from orange paper (HC) using grooves 2 and 3 of the Coluzzle template and stick it on the card. Punch out the carts, the fences and the canoes from different colours of Happy Color card. Stick the carts on top of each other on the left-hand side of the card and put the bears in the cart. Punch out seven balloons and stick one letter from the word "Holiday" on each balloon. Use a white pen to draw the strings. Use eyelets to attach both sides of the fence to the card. Stick another couple of bears on the card. Stick the canoes on top of each other and stick two ropes to the canoe. Use eyelets with star shapes to attach the ropes to the card. Also add a couple of eyelets with star shapes around the canoe. Stick the bears in the canoe. Stick the background scene in the middle of the dark green card. Finally, stick the inner card in the outer card.

4. Long live the holidays

Make a crimson double card (15 x 13 cm). Cut a piece of ivory card (15 x 13 cm) and punch a decorative border in the top. Make a mountain fold in the middle and a valley fold 5 cm from this fold on both sides. Punch the trees out of jungle paper and stick them on the card. Cut the strengthened animals out and use eyelets to connect the tails and, for the monkey, the arms. Use an eyelet to hang the monkey in the tree. Stick the other animals on the card using a couple of pieces of foam tape. Colour the text sticker green using the Identi-pen and stick it on the card. Finally, stick the card in the outer card.

Nice big cards

You can really surprise someone with a lovely, big card.

What you need:

- ❏ *Cutting sheets: nos. S2301, S2306, S2309 and E2310*
- ❏ *Card: 33 x 16.5 cm – sunny yellow (A247), pastel blue (A413), black (A219), red (A519), royal blue (A427), bright yellow (C400) and bright red (C506)*
- ❏ *Piece of carnival red card (HC03)*
- ❏ *Alphabet punch set*
- ❏ *Eyelets, shapes and toolkit*
- ❏ *Photo corner figure punch: curl and heart*
- ❏ *Alphabet silhouette stencil*
- ❏ *Background stamp and white stamp-pad ink*
- ❏ *Memory cutting sheet: rusk with aniseed comfits*

1. Party

Cut part of the royal blue card (33 x 16.5 cm) away at an angle so that there is 6 cm left at the top and 13 cm at the bottom. Stamp the pattern on the card using the background stamp and white stamp-pad ink. Stick the yellow card inside the blue card. Use eyelets to connect the strengthened parts of the children together. Use one eyelet to attach each child to the yellow part of the card, so that they can tumble and rotate on the card and their arms and legs can be moved into any position you wish. Stick the kite and the dog on the card. Add a couple of eyelets and star shapes. Cut out the letters "PARTY" using the silhouette stencil and stick them on the yellow part of the card.

2. Many congratulations

Cut two 3 cm wide strips and two 2.5 cm wide strips from the red card. Cut a yellow card (16.5 x 16.5 cm) and stick this inside the card. Stick the strips you have cut off on this card, leaving a small gap between each strip. Strengthen the parts of the cutting sheet and cut them out. Cut the head and the bow into separate parts. Use pink eyelets to connect the head of the donkey together. Stick the head of the donkey to the card using photo glue and use yellow eyelets to attach the ears to the inside of the card. Stick the bow on the card. Make an incision in the card just above the bow and insert the neck through this so that the mouth can move. Use orange eyelets to stick the hoofs on the card. Punch out the letters "Many congratulations" using the alphabet punch and stick them on the card.

3. Baby card

Cut a 3.5 cm wide strip from the front of the pastel blue card (33 x 16.5 cm). Cut out the scene with the stork and stick it on the card. Cut the card away from the dog, around the stork, to the baby bottle. Use eyelets to attach the strengthened wings to the back of the stork. Also attach the cords which are used to move the wings and thread a couple of beads on them. Make the stork 3D. Cut the part with the rusk and aniseed comfits (15.5 x 12 cm) from the Memory cutting sheet and stick this against the inside of the card. Use the heart photo corner punch to make a dark blue punched border. Add the eyelets and heart shapes to the border of the card. The stork will *fly* if you pull the cord.

4. The strong man

Make a black card (30 x 15 cm). Cut a piece of red card (14 x 14 cm) and punch out the corners using the photo corner punch. Cut a piece of yellow card (13 x 13 cm). Strengthen the parts of the strong man and use eyelets to attach the bar to the shoulders. Use eyelets to attach the knees and the weights to the yellow card. Make all the parts 3D. Slide the yellow card into the red card and stick everything on the black card using small strips of double-sided adhesive tape.

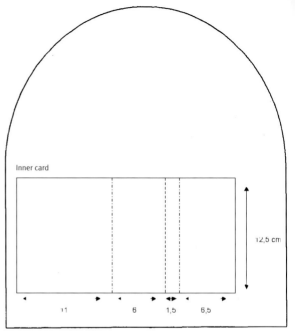

Inner card

12,5 cm

11 6 1,5 6,5

Actual size window (for card on page 1)

Card pattern for the card on page 1

Outer card

12,5 cm

12,5 cm

25 cm

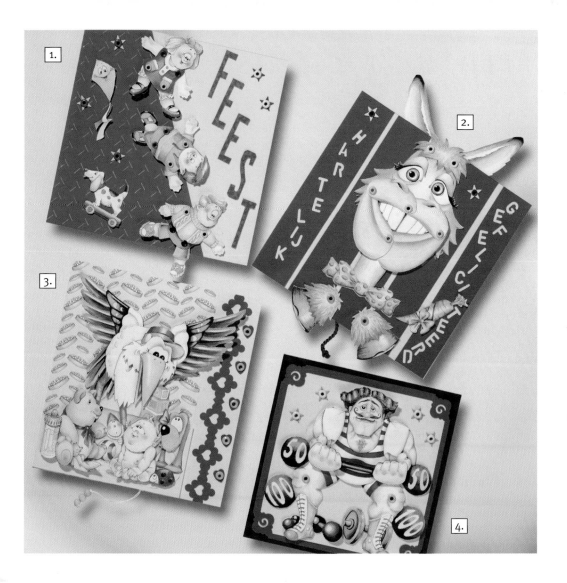

1.

2.

3.

4.

Triptych cards

Special cards with colourful bows.

What you need:
- ❑ Gallery cards: ornament (x 2) and wave (x 4) (Kars)
- ❑ Cutting sheets: nos. S2302, S2305, S2307, S2308 and E2314
- ❑ Eyelets: blue, pink, red, yellow and flower shapes
- ❑ Eyelets toolkit
- ❑ Stamp-pad ink (blue and green), sponge
- ❑ Decorative ribbon: blue, white and red

General information

You need two pieces of the same card for the triptych cards. Cut one Gallery card through the middle. Cut about 3 cm off of the bottom of the cards. Sponge the cards with blue stamp-pad ink making a rotating movement from top to bottom and with green ink from the bottom to the top. Place the part you have cut off at the bottom of the card, use a pencil to mark the holes and use the hollow pipe to punch new holes in the card.

1. Bears in a boat

Add red eyelets to the holes in the card. Cut the parts out of cutting sheet S2307. Strengthen the boat and the ropes with 160 gram card. Stick the background with the tree to the middle part of the card. Use the hollow pipe to punch holes at the indicated positions on the different parts and use eyelets to connect them together. Make the tree and the boat 3D. Cut the background and the bears in the boat out again. Cut the tree through the middle and stick one half on each side of the card. Stick the bears slightly behind the trees. Make the top of the tree 3D. Tie the different parts of the card together using the red decorative ribbon.

2. Bathing ladies

Add blue eyelets to the holes in the card. Strengthen the parts of the ladies and cut them out. Stick the background to the middle part of the card. Use the hollow pipe to make holes at the indicated positions on the different parts you have cut out and use eyelets to connect them together (see the cutting sheet). The ladies in the bathing costumes can now move. Puff up the heads of the ladies and stick them on the necks using a large drop of silicon glue. Make the rest 3D. Cut the windbreak, the life buoy, the beach huts, the sunglasses and the sea-gull out of cutting sheet E2314 and stick them on the left and right-hand sides of the card. Tie the parts of the card together using the blue decorative ribbon.

3. The first kiss

Add pink eyelets to the holes in the card. Cut the parts out of cutting sheet S2305. Strengthen the children and the bar with 160 gram card. Stick the background on the middle part of the card. Use the hollow pipe to make holes at the indicated positions on the different parts you have cut out and use eyelets to connect them together. The children can now move back and forth and kiss each other. Make the scene 3D. Cut the background out of cutting sheet S2305. Cut it through the middle and stick it on both sides of the card. Punch a yellow eyelet with a flower shape in the flowers. Tie the parts of the card together using the white decorative ribbon.

Continued from page 31

4. Baby in a flower basket
Cut a piece of light blue card (100 gram, 13 x 10 cm). Punch the flower border using the border punch. Open the dark blue card and use cream eyelets and blue flower shapes to attach the light blue card to it. Also add a line of three flowers to the dark blue card. Punch the flower basket out of dark blue card and use a cream eyelet to attach a strengthened baby's head to the handle. The eyelet allows the head to rotate. Stick the flowers in the flower basket and make them 3D. Thread the blue ribbon through the eyelets and tie it into a bow.

A day out

The things that can happen on a day out.

What you need:
- ❏ Cutting sheets: S2303, S2304, S2305 and E2315
- ❏ Card: 26 x 13 cm – red (A517) and birch green (A305)
- ❏ Card: 25 x 12.5 cm – royal blue (HC05), carnival red (HC03) and sea green (HC04); A4 – bright yellow (C400) and azure (C590)
- ❏ Eyelets, shapes and toolkit
- ❏ Coluzzle template: drop
- ❏ Medium punch (sun)
- ❏ Figure scissors
- ❏ Vellum
- ❏ Background stamp, white stamp-pad ink
- ❏ Knitting needle and Wire & Wire 26 gauge wire

Sizzix die-cutter

A large number of dies are available for the Sizzix die-cutter. I have used some attractive dies with this tool and, together with the Marij cutting sheets, they make the cards really pretty.
Use the die-cutter as follows:
Take a piece of card of your choice and place it on the white pad. Place the die on top of the card and feed it bit by bit through the die-cutter. Pull the lever down a couple of times to produce a nice cut.
Tip: if you do not have the die-cutter, ask your shopkeeper for the dies.

Funny car (see photograph on page 3)

Cut a piece of vellum (13 x 13 cm) and use two eyelets to attach it to the card. Strengthen the pieces of the cutting sheet and use eyelets to connect all the pieces together (see the cutting sheet). Make everything 3D. Use one eyelet to attach the car to the card and use eyelets and flower shapes to decorate the corners of the card.

1. On the boat

Tear a couple of wavy strips from the piece of vellum. Place them slightly on top of each other and use two blue eyelets to attach them to the royal blue card. Cut the sailing boat out of carnival red card. Cut the funny family out, cut them through the middle and glue one part of the family behind the sail and one part in front of the sail. Use a red eyelet to attach the boat's flag to the card. Cut the boat out again and stick only the bottom part on the card using a couple of pieces of foam tape. Decorate the card with eyelets and star shapes.

2. *Many congratulations*
Stamp the pattern on the red card using the background stamp and the white stamp-pad ink. Tear a fancy road surface from yellow paper and stick it on the bottom of the card. Cut the funny car out and place red eyelets in the wheels. Stick the car on the card using a couple of pieces of foam tape. Strengthen the animals. Use eyelets to attach their tails and stick them in the car. Use an eyelet to hang the monkey on the car. Use the Coluzzle template to cut the labels and use eyelets and cord to attach them to the card. Stick the text on the labels.

3. *Rodeo pig*
Cut a piece of vellum (12.5 x 12.5 cm). Use four pink eyelets and red heart shapes to attach it to the carnival red card. Use eyelets to connect the pieces of the rodeo pig together (see the cutting sheet) and use one pink eyelet to attach it to the card. The moveable handle is slid through the opening in the card. And now, let's see if the clown can stay on.

4. *Fishing along the water's edge*
Cut a thin strip from the green card using figure scissors. Cut a piece of blue card (13 x 13 cm) and stick this inside the card. Cut a piece of vellum (13 x 6 cm) and use two yellow eyelets and flower shapes to attach it to the card. Cut the background from the cutting sheet and stick it on the green card (partly behind the vellum). Strengthen the gnome. Use an eyelet to attach the arms and use an eyelet to attach it to the card (see the cutting sheet). Twist a long, thin spiral around a knitting needle and attach it to the fishing rod and the strengthened boot. Stick the fish in the bottom corner. Punch the suns out and use eyelets and cord to attach them to the card.

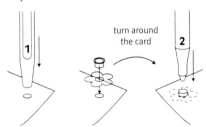

turn around the card

Adding eyelets

Folded cards

Nice, small cards to put on display.

What you need:
- ❏ *Cutting sheets: nos. S2300, S2303, E 2313 and 2315*
- ❏ *Card: A5 – carnival red (HC03), sea green (HC04) and royal blue (HC05)*
- ❏ *Card: pink (C352), blue (C490) and almond green (C480)*
- ❏ *Eyelets and toolkit*
- ❏ *Sticker sheet with white texts and white borders*

General information
Fold the card according to the diagram on page 30. Use the folding tool to produce nice, sharp mountain and valley folds, so that the card can be easily pushed into shape. Cut a piece of Canson card (7 x 7 cm) in a suitable colour and use two or four eyelets to attach it to the folded card. Fold the card open so that you can attach the eyelets. Use a piece of foam tape or double-sided adhesive tape to stick the sides together.

1. Red baby card
Cut a piece of pink card (7 x 7 cm). Use pink eyelets to attach the strengthened baby and the head to the card. Use two pink eyelets to attach the card to the red folded card and add a white decorative border. Stick a flower and heart shapes on the right-hand side of the card and use an eyelet to attach a strengthened baby's head on top of this. Add a text sticker.

2. Green card with a clown
Cut a piece of light green card (7 x 7 cm). Cut out the strengthened clown and connect the pieces together using an eyelet. Make the clown's head 3D and use an eyelet to attach the clown to the card. Use yellow eyelets to attach the card to the green background and add a white decorative border. Stick the raised up bunch of flowers on the right-hand side of the card and add a text sticker under it.

3. Blue baby card
Cut a piece of light blue card (7 x 7 cm). Stick the strengthened baby's body on the card and stick the baby's head on top of it. Use two light blue eyelets to attach the card to the blue background and add a white decorative border. Stick the corner flower pattern on the left-hand side and add a text sticker.

4. Green card with a lion
Cut a piece of light green card (7 x 7 cm). Cut out the strengthened lion and use a brown eyelet to connect the tail. Stick the lion on the card using a couple of pieces of foam tape and use brown eyelets to attach this card to the green background. Cut the box out and stick it under the lion. Stick the mouse on the stool on the right-hand side and add a text sticker.

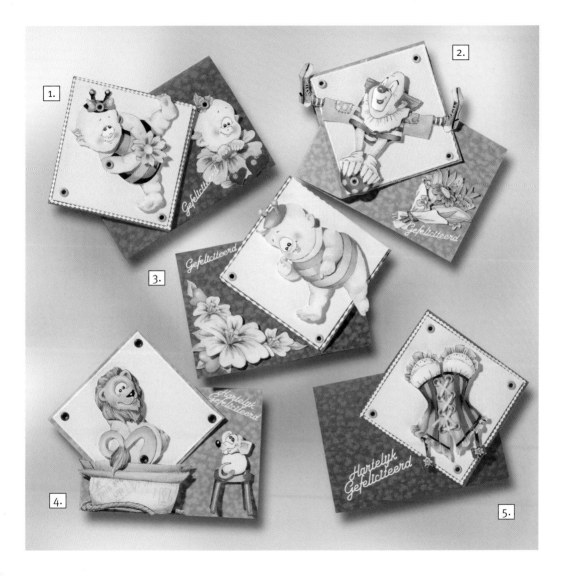

5. Red card with a corset.

Cut a piece of pink card (7 x 7 cm). Cut out the strengthened corset. Add the eyelets in the places indicated and thread a yellow cord through them. Stick the corset on the card using a couple of pieces of foam tape. Use four eyelets to attach the card to the red background. Add a text sticker on the left-hand side.

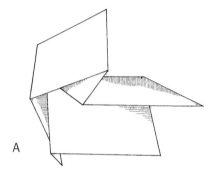

A

Folded card

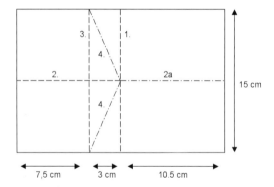

3.   1.

4.

2.   2a

15 cm

7,5 cm   3 cm   10.5 cm

Valley fold _ _ _ _ _ _ _ _
(fold towards yourself)

Mountain fold _.._.._.._.._
(fold away from yourself)

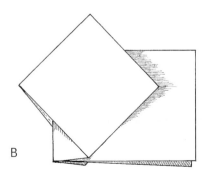

B

Babies and elves

A congratulatory card is always suitable for a birth. Maybe one of these?

What you need:
- ❑ Cutting sheets: S2306 and E2313
- ❑ Card : 26 x 13 cm – azure (A 393), dark blue (A 427) and pink (A481)
- ❑ Card: A4 – blue (C490)
- ❑ 100 gram card: 13 x 13 – light blue (A413)
- ❑ Vellum: pink baby bottles and flower fairies
- ❑ Line border flower punch
- ❑ Double corner punch (flower)
- ❑ Sizzix die-cutter and die (flower basket)
- ❑ Eyelets, shapes and toolkit
- ❑ Hexagon Coluzzle template
- ❑ Wire & Wire 26 gauge wire, ribbon

1. Blue card with elves

Cut a piece of dark blue card (12.8 x 12.8 cm). Punch out the corners and stick it on the azure card. Cut a hexagon out of light blue card using the Coluzzle template and add blue eyelets in the corners. Stick the card on the dark blue card. Decorate the border using border stickers. Strengthen the baby's head and the baby with wings. Cut out the flower pot and stick it on the light blue part of the card. Make the flower border 3D. Use an eyelet to attach the baby's head just above the flowers. Also use eyelets to attach the wings. Attach the left wing directly to the card.

2. Stork with a baby

Cut a piece of vellum (13 x 7.5 cm) and use pink eyelets to attach it to the pink card. Strengthen the head of the stork and the baby. Use a pink eyelet to attach the head of the stork to the vellum. Twist a spiral around a knitting needle and stick it behind the baby using adhesive tape. Stick the other end to the stork's beak using a piece of foam tape. Decorate the card. Thread the pink ribbon through the eyelets and tie it into a bow.

3. Flower fairies

Cut a piece of vellum (13 x 13 cm) and use pink eyelets and ivory flower shapes to attach it to the pink card. Strengthen the parts of the baby. Use eyelets to connect the parts together and stick the baby on the card. Make the baby 3D. Use an eyelet to attach the flowers to the card. Thread the pink ribbon through the eyelets and tie it into a bow.

Continued on page 23

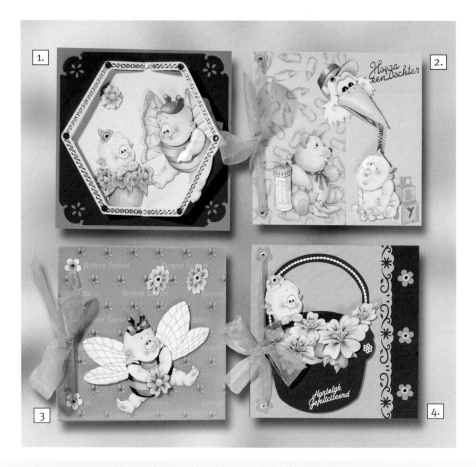

With thanks to Kars, Ochten, the Netherlands, for supplying the materials.

The materials used can be ordered by shopkeepers from:
Kars & Co BV, Ochten, the Netherlands
Also see my website: www.betsylurvink.nl